Proverbial Wisdom from Guyana

by

Victorine Grannum-Solomon

Dedication

This book is dedicated to the memory of my mother
Winifred Willings Grannum, who spent tireless hours
teaching her children to ensure they were literate.
Also, to the memory of my daughter Ama Lebone, who
for a short while brought her light into our world.
And, to my children Njeri, Ecua and Kwesi, in the hope
that it will enrich their experience with the proverbial
aspect of their Guyanese culture.

Contents

Foreword

Proverbial Wisdom from Guyana is a welcome addition to the growing collection of works on the language of Guyana and the Caribbean. It represents a valuable contribution to the furtherance of the
study of creole linguistics, and its appearance at a time contempora-
neous with a *Dictionary of Caribbean English Usage* by Allsopp, at
the turn of a new century, is somehow portentous. It is not merely
a matter of "passing of a milestone" since the historic and seminal
conference, *Festival of Guyanese Words*, which was organized by the
University of Guyana in the 1970's. Indeed, the work done by Mrs.
Solomon marks a certain "coming of age" in the specialized area of
creole linguistics.

The book is at once entertaining and informative, and it places at
our finger tips, in a manageable form, the wide range of sayings and
aphorisms which make up the body of wisdom handed down to us
over the ages by our ancestors. At the same time across the narra-
tive, and piercing through the analyses, are the reflections of the
peculiar style and the remarkable vision of the world that are truly
Caribbean.

Professor J. Loncke
University of Guyana

Preface

In this proverbial collection an insight is given into the thoughts, feelings, and experiences of the people from Guyana. Proverbs are viewed as strategies for dealing with situations and are therefore categorized in these pages under the headings Advice, Warning, Threat, Encouragement, Indifference, and Criticism. Some of the proverbs are given in context, since context facilitates the production of proverbs. It is hoped that readers will be entranced by the ring of wisdom endemic to these proverbs.

This collection does not include every proverb that exists, but it does contain some of the most widely used proverbs in Guyana today. It is within the frequently used proverb that one can find what Guyanese people regard as true, as well as much of their general dispositions toward the world. Since they are rooted in an oral tradition, scholars have been hesitant to record them because there is no standard orthography for the transcription. However, even in the absence of a standard orthography for creole languages, it is important to document this aspect of our Guyanese culture.

This book is aimed at the Guyanese living both at home and abroad who want to reappraise their cultural roots. However, it is hoped that many others—of Caribbean, African, and African-American descent, in addition to students of folklore and black studies in general—will find this collection of interest. This aspect of Guyana's culture is important not only for the people from Guyana but also for all Africans in the diaspora. Proverbial knowledge belongs not only to our past and present but also to our future. Yesterday, today, and tomorrow are one process. To cut one off from the other is to tek basket fo fetch water (to take a basket to fetch or carry water.)

Victorine Grannum-Solomon

Acknowledgments

The nucleus of this book comes from a project completed as part of the requirements for a bachelor's degree decades ago. To those persons who were the sources of the material used in that project I owe a special gratitude. They were Kwame Apata, George Young, Wordsworth McAndrew, "Aunt Ruth," and "Tunde." In addition, my gratitude goes out to George Cave, who stimulated my interest in creole language studies and who guided me through that nucleus project. To all those Guyanese who have since indulged my interest in proverb collection I owe a special thanks. I am also indebted to my husband, Cyril (Bradley) Solomon, who provided me with encouragement and constructive suggestions for improving the text.

I am alone responsible, however, for the views contained in this book; any shortcomings or errors derive from my limitations.

Victorine Grannum-Solomon

Introduction

Guyanese proverbial expressions are a reflection of the wit, wisdom, and philosophy of the people from Guyana. These allusive, metaphorical images of our values are both an art form and an educational tool. Many of them were formulated by the uprooted Africans as a code of conduct, as a set of mores for living in a new society. In Guyana today, proverbs are used extensively in the daily life of the folk to inculcate morality, to teach values, and to instill acceptable modes of conduct.

There are basically two sources of proverbial wisdom. There is that of the common man, whose proverbial utterances, which are transmitted as an oral tradition, are concrete fragments of wisdom and the result of observation. There is also that of the "wise man" or oracle, whose utterances were the result of reflection and wisdom. These were usually received by the folk who did not have the time or mental capacity to meditate upon fundamental truths. Some of the Guyanese Creole proverbs fall into the first category. They are the sententious sayings of the old Africans to whom abstract thought could best be expressed by means of the concrete situations familiar to them. From the connotation of some of these proverbs it appears as though they might have arisen during the plantation system. Many of those are not much heard today. For example, *sometin mo dan keen mek ii ton shugo* (something more than cane made it turn into sugar). This proverb tells of the sweat, blood, and the great amount of energy, both human and mechanical, which came between the cane in the field and the sugar on the market.

One of the most striking features of Guyanese Creole proverbs is the allusion to animal life. No one can fail to observe the frequent references to animals, insects, fish, birds, and reptiles. In Guyana the people live close to nature; hence, images from nature inform their lives. The habits and peculiarities of animals are highlighted, and allusions are made to human characteristics in an effort to assist humans in learning from the proverbs.

The animal images used convey a vivid picture and focus the meaning of the proverb on the minds of the folk. "Animal life plays a large part in the symbolism of these sayings. Dog, *daag*, symbolizes the poor man and monkey, *monkii*, the senseless one."[1] In the proverbs, *maaga* has all the connotations of lean, skinny, and hungry. In Guyanese creolese, a *dressa* is usually a kitchen table on which meals are kept; it usually houses things needed to prepare the daily meals. It is, therefore, possible that when the *dressa* falls down the *magga daag* will get something to eat. *Maaga daag* could then be used to symbolize the poor, unfortunate man who laughs at a better man's misfortune if he stands to gain. However, although animal images are used, the proverbs have a more didactic meaning when applied to man.

In this collection the proverbs are viewed as strategies for dealing with situations and are therefore categorized as: Advice, Warning, Threat, Encouragement, Indifference, and Criticism. However, these divisions are far from being precise since context must be used as the basis for interpretation of the proverbs. It is the very nature of a good proverb that it says so many things at once, that it cannot always easily be put into any clear-cut category.

In examining the proverbs, some seem to be either an advice or a warning depending on the context of situation. For example, a father in trying to put his wayward son on the right path may advise him that, *muun a ron til dee kech am*. The son must desist from indulging in illicit and/or illegal activities. However, the young man who is continually being accosted by a bully may warn him with the same proverb. One day he means to get even. Meaning can, therefore, only be derived from the context of the situation in which the proverb is placed. In like manner, many of the proverbs dealing with encouragement if placed in specific contexts could be sources of advice.

In others, not only context of situation but also emphasis on certain words play important parts in determining meaning. For example: *Piknii wa na heer ii muma ii a fiil* (The child who does not hear his mother will feel). Let us assume that a little boy was playing with a box of matches. The mother saw, took them away, and told him not to interfere with them again. Five minutes later she saw him with the matches again and told him, picknii wa na heer muma ii a fiil." She used this proverb with equal stress on all syllables. However, about ten minutes later she again caught him with the matches. In a loud voice she told him
"Piknii wa na^heer mu-ma ii a ^fiil "
Here I adopted the device of varying the level of the words to indicate differences of stress. If emphasis is placed on the words heer, fiil, and the syllable ma, the proverb becomes a warning. The parent is no longer advising the child but warning him.

In rendering many of the proverbs, Guyanese frequently use paralinguistic features, such as facial expressions and gestures. These help to communicate ideas vividly.

In many Guyanese Creole proverbs, repetition is used either for emphasis or to signify habitual use. The device of repositioning of phrase is also used for a more telling impact. For example: *If yu fain a gool brooch a daans haal, a daans haal yu gu laas am* (If you find a gold broach in the dance hall, in this dance hall you will lose it). The phrase *a daans haal* is repeated to emphasize the particular place in which the broach will be lost. However, in the proverb like, *Horii horii mek baad korii* (Hurry, hurry made bad curry), which suggests that excessive hurrying may have negative results, the significant words are *horii, horii*. It is not *horii* which is bad, but excessive hurrying. In the example, *Plee, plee a bring nee, nee*

(Play, play will bring nay, nay), the suggestion is that excessive play may lead to tears. Again, it is not play but excessive playing which might have serious repercussions. *Nee, nee,* which seems to have its origin in neigh, the horses cry, signifies tears. The folk speech, it would appear, has a special affinity for words involving sound play, reduplication or iteration, and onomatopoeic words.

Another major feature of Guyanese Creole proverbs is that they incorporate the device of negation. This aspect of negation corresponds to the fact that in the Guyanese social structure the subordinate group largely in the rural areas use a great deal of proverbs when instructing the young. If the proverbs in this collection are examined, the frequency of *na* meaning "do not" or "did not," seems to abound in all categories but moreover in proverbs dealing with advice.

For example, a Guyanese Father of the subordinate group may say to his child, *Reen a faal bukit na ful juu kyaan ful am* (If the rain fell and the bucket was not filled then dew cannot fill it). This may be used in a situation in which a teenager neglects to prepare for an examination despite being advised to study by his parents. As time for the examination draws near, he proceeds to make a last-minute effort to prepare for the examination. The parent may say, *reen a faal bukit na ful juu kyaan ful am.* This advises one to use great efforts to achieve results; otherwise when a little effort is used one must fail. This proverb in which two negatives are used is representative of the abundance of negation used in proverbs dealing with advice. The Guyanese social structure allows for an abundant use of negatives among the subordinate class. This is in direct contrast to the type of negation used by the superordinate group.

People traditionally have been led to believe that the creole language[2] is bad or broken English. Persons who speak it are taught to be inferior both socially and economically. Many educated Guyanese, therefore, engage frequently in code switching and other changes in communicative styles and strategies depending on the formality or informality of one's conversation. Guyanese creolese proverbs as expressions of the folk culture serve the main function of language which is to communicate. It is by language that humans transmit their thoughts, attitudes, and activities to other humans. Proverbs as aspect of language, therefore, gives a glimpse of the workings of the folk mind.

Another feature of the proverbs is the distinctive use of tense. Since Guyanese Creole is a distinctly different system from standard English, it adopts its own devices for expressing different states of being in the present, past, and future time.
A brief discussion will center around tense in the proverbs.

In Guyanese Creole, *a* is used as a marker for both present and future to express ideas which would be rendered by *be* in standard language. As a present aspectual marker, *a* can refer to the present tense. For example, *sin a beer blasom* translates to sin is bearing blossoms. *A* can also express futurity, as in *yu a gu miit am*: you will meet it. To express the present tense, Guyanese Creole uses the base form of the verb with *ing* or the base form of the verb alone. For Example: *shi ronin* (she is running) or *dem taakin* (they are talking). In the above examples, the copula are and is are omitted. Absence of copula, or the verb to be is a feature of many Creole languages and also a feature of Ebonics.

If the action is continuing in the present, Guyanese Creole uses the present marker *a* with the base form of the word, as in the example *shi a ron* or *dem a taak*. Since *a* is the auxiliary which expresses continuous action, it is often used in proverbs.

To express past tense or time, Guyanese Creole uses the basic form of the verb alone, as in *shi ron* or *dem taak*. Since this construction is also used for the present tense, the context in which it is used determines the meaning. This form of the language is also similar to Ebonics, where the same verb form can express present and past tense.

To express futurity, Guyanese Creole use a number of devices. Among these are: *gon, gun, gu, gin, goin, gwine, gain* with the base form of the form verb would be. An example is shi gu ron or dem gu taak. To express future aspect, Guyanese Creole use the marker a with *gu* and the base form of the verb, such as *shi a gu ron* or *dem a gu taak*.

To express completed aspect in the future, Guyanese Creole use *bina* plus the base form of the verb. For example, *shi bina gu ron* or *dem bina gu taak*. It is also true that Guyanese Creole use several devices with a, *bin*, and *bina* to express different aspects of time. However, since *bin* and *bina* express past concepts, they are not used in Guyanese Creole proverbs, which express only continuous ideas.

Similarities to Caribbean and West African proverbs

In studying the proverbs, it was observed that Guyanese Creole proverbs bear similarity to other Caribbean proverbs and also to some West African proverbs. This fact seems to support a theory that the Africans who were uprooted from their civilization in Africa brought their proverbial ideas to the Caribbean, and related them to their new surroundings. It also supports the theory that some of the Guyanese proverbs have their origins in African proverbs. Anyone familiar with the theories concerning the development of Guyanese Creole would be aware that African languages influenced all Caribbean Creoles.

The following chart adopted from Cave (72) illustrates his theory, a monogenetic one, of how Guyanese Creole developed. From the chart, it is apparent that other English–based Caribbean Creoles and Ebonics developed under parallel lines to Guyanese Creole. Because of affinities both in grammatical structure and in the lexis of Caribbean Creoles, linguists developed the theory of parallel development and common genetic ancestor. These Caribbean Creoles tended to derive most of their vocabulary from a given European language, depending on the European power(s) which dominated their territory.

Cave's Chart showing Development of Guyanese Creole

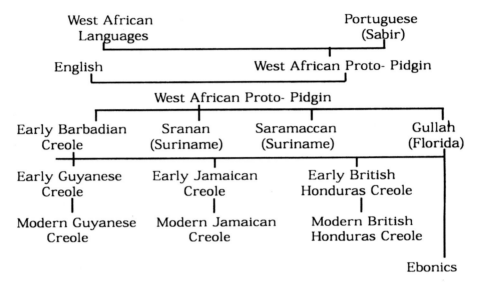

Parallel threads are observed not only in the development of the languages, but in identical proverbs that are found in Caribbean and West African societies. In addition, when Caribbean proverbs are examined, some are found to have parallels in Guyanese Creole proverbs. These parallel trends seem to suggest that they were derived from the same source. For example, the Guyana proverb, "man dead grass grow at his door" is rendered in Jamaica and Trinidad as, "man dead grass grow at his door mouth." This proverb means that as long as authority is absent, subordinates do what they please.

The Guyana proverb, "if man does not like you he will give you a basket to carry water," is rendered in Jamaica as, "if man hates you, he will give you fork to drink soup and a basket to carry water," and in Trinidad as "never give a man basket to carry water." Another Guyanese proverb, "moon runs until day catches it," is rendered in Jamaica as "moon does run but day does catch him." The proverb means that the disobedient child will meet with misfortune.

Guyanese say, "The pickney who does not hear his mother will feel." A Trinidad equivalent says, "pickney who does not hear his mother will have to drink hot water without sugar." The Guyanese saying, "do not take a bird if you do not have cage," is rendered in Trinidad as, "get cage before you get bird." This proverb advises one to make adequate preparations before undertaking a venture.

Another Guyanese proverb which says, "jail was not made for dogs," is rendered in Trinidad as, "goal was not made for dogs." It is frequently put forward by a person as a show of bravado, when in fact the person is ashamed for having been to jail.

Another Guyanese maxim says, "do not see something in the day and take a fire-stick to look for it in the night." Trinidadians, on the other hand, have an equivalent proverb which says "only a fool will see something in day time, and take fire-stick to look for it in the night." This proverb means that it is unwise to be in a position to achieve something good, spurn that opportunity, and then strive after the same good when circumstances are very disadvantageous.

Similarities are, however, not limited to Caribbean proverbs. They are also seen between Caribbean proverbs and West African proverbs. One must recall that the English and the French conducted most of their trading activities on the West African coast. The slaves who were brought to the Caribbean must have related their habit of conceptualization in Africa to their new Caribbean environment. It must also be noted that the slaves who were brought to Guyana spoke many languages: Yoruba, Fante, Twi, Congo, Assante, Ewe, and Mande, to name a few. Guyanese proverbs would have been influenced by proverbs from different languages or regions. Below are some African proverbs which resemble some Guyanese and Caribbean Creole proverbs, in lexis, structure and concept. The sources from which the proverbs are derived are indicated. The African proverbs appeared in Beckwith's work.

The Guyanese maxim, "the stone at the bottom of the river does not know how the sun is hot," is rendered in Nigeria, as, "the stone in the water does not know how hot the hill is parched by the sun." Jamaicans, on the other hand, say "rock stone at the river-bottom never feel sun hot. The concept behind this proverb is that the rich never know the discomfort of the poor.

Another West African proverb says, "the young wild hog asked his mother, 'mama what are the warts in thy face?' She replied, 'by and by thou wilt have seen it already.'" This is rendered in Guyana as, "pig asked his mother what made her mouth long so, mother said, 'wait you are growing you will meet it.'" A Jamaican equivalent is rendered as, "pig ask him mother say what make him mouth long so; him say, take time my pickney; that something make for me long so, will make for you long so too.'" The essence of the proverb is that one should not laugh at another's misfortune, because it is possible that one suffers in the same way.

Parallels are also seen in the Guyana proverb, "when the cat is not there the rat takes over." This is rendered in Hausa as "the cat in not at home because of that the mice are playing." In Ahanti it is rendered as, "when the cat dies the mice rejoices." This proverb suggests that when authority is absent, subordinates are happy and so do what they please.

xiii

The Tanzania saying, "everything has an end," is not very different from Guyanese: "the longest rope has an end." These proverbs suggest that nothing last forever. The Guyanese proverb, "even the night have ears," and "bush have ears," is rendered in Tanzania as, "even flies have ears."

An Ashanti proverb says that, "when you go to the rat's house and he eats palm nut kernels you eat some too." The Guyanese equivalent is "when you go to the country where the people are dancing with one foot dance with one foot too." The Guyanese maxim "one finger cannot pick a louse," is rendered in Swahili as, "one finger will not kill a louse."

The Hausa proverb, "if the fish comes out of the water and says the eyes of the crocodile are one in number, who is going to argue with him?" is similar to the Accra proverb, "if an Apopokiki from the bottom of the river says that the crocodile is sick, then it is truly sick." These parallel the Guyanese, "if patwa come out of trench bottom and say huri is there believe him." Jamaicans on the other hand have a similar proverb which says, "if the fish comes out of the sea and tells you that alligator have fever believe him." This proverb means one should listen to those in a better position to offer advise.

From the examples, it can be seen that parallel trends seem to characterize many West African and Caribbean proverbs. These African proverbs which I have given are peculiar to different tribes. Earlier, I mentioned some of the tribes and regions from which slaves were brought to Guyana. Some of the Guyanese Creole proverbs under study have identical members, as was shown with those found in West Africa. This evidence seems to suggest that the Africans who were uprooted brought their proverbial knowledge with them and related the same concepts to their new surroundings.

In summary, Guyanese Creole proverbs bear not only structural similarities to other proverbs in the African diaspora; but linguistically, they share affinities to other Creole languages and to Ebonics. Like other African influenced languages, characteristics of these proverbs include: tonal variations, use of double and triple negatives, and the use of repetition. The language also has a special affinity for words involving sound play, reduplication or iteration, and onomatopoeic words. Stress, intonation, other subtle nuances of the language, and the use of paralinguistic features or nonverbal communication are other features. These proverbs are also rich in imagery and metaphor, and are able to give a vivid picture in few words. Like other Creole languages and Ebonics, the verb to be is not conjugated.

Guyanese Creole proverbs, like Creole languages all over the world, were passed down through an oral tradition. African descendants in Guyana seemed to have used the oral tradition similar to that which was used by the GRIOTS in passing customs down to their descendants. In this way, the proverbs came down through the ages.

xiv

System of Transcription

The orthography used for transcribing the creole proverb is a simplified version of the script adopted by Cassidy (1961). This system has the advantage of being phonemic, of being consistent, and of requiring the use of no diacritics. The consonants, vowels and diphthongs used in this system are as follows:

Consonants

b - bad *bad*   m - man *man*   y - yes *yes*
d - dog *dog*   n - noon *nuun*   z - zoo *zuu*
f - fan *fan*   p - pin *pin*   sh - ship *ship*
g - gun *gon*   r - rat *rats*   ch - charm *chaarm*
h - hot *hot*   s - sat *sat*   th - that *that*
j - jam *jam*   t - tin *tin*   ng - sing *sing*
K - keep *kiip*   v - very *verii*   nk - think *think*
l - lad *lad*   w - want *want*   zk - pleasure *plezhor*

Vowels

a - hat *hat*
aa - art *aart*
e - bet *bet*
ee - able *eebl*
i - it *it*

Dipthongs

ai - side *said*   ii - eat *iit*
ou - about *about*   o - come *kom*
ea - stair *stear*   oo - only *oonli*
oi - boys *boiz*   u - good *gud*
                        uu - fool *fuul*

This collection is not meant to be a comprehensive one of the proverbs in existence; however, it contains some of the most pervasive proverbs in Guyana today. Further, other collections of Guyanese proverbs do exist. These include Speirs, The Proverbs of British Guiana (1902); Allsop, Folklore in Guiana; (1967), Abrams, Guyana Mete Gee; (1970), Lawrence, Interpretations of Commonly Used Guyanese Creolese Proverbs; (1972), Solomon A Study of Guyanese Creole Proverbs (1974), and Kwayana, gang gang (1997). In addition, individual scholars may well have small collections of proverbs in papers and unpublished theses. However, no major collection on the subject has been published for several decades. This book is an attempt to preserve and make accessible a vital part of the Guyanese culture which is a neglected field of scholarship.

A Word about Sources and the Collection Of Proverbs

In the remainder of this book, three versions of each proverb are given. First each proverb is expressed in creolese. This is followed by a literal translation, and then the meaning of the proverb is given. The entire book is divided into six parts: Advice, Warning, Threat, Encouragement, Indifference, and Criticism. Each part of the book is preceded by a brief introduction intended to assist the reader in assimilating the essence of the proverb in context.

Some of the proverbs in the present collection were collected by the author some years ago while working on a thesis on Guyanese Creole Proverbs. Informants were Kwame Apata, George Younge, Wordsworth McAndrew, "Aunt Ruth," and "Tunde". Other material was collected by the author over a number of years from informal sources. Some of the informants had given the contexts in which the proverbs were used; other meanings were supplied by the author and her husband.

Advice

Children are highly valued in the Guyanese community, and proverbs are used as a means of transmitting values and encouraging appropriate behavior. In exercising authority over children, parents, elders, and other siblings use proverbs as didactic markers. These proverbs, which are primarily instructive, are used as a measure of social control, as a behavior management technique; or as an educational tool. The chief function of this type of proverb is to make the listener look introspectively at his behavior; to weigh decisions before acting; and to invoke a kind of reflective, pensive mood in the listener before pursuing their actions.

In the Guyanese context, the family refers not only to the nuclear family (which is made up of husband, wife, and children) but also may contain one or more members of one's extended family (grandparents, grandchildren, uncles, aunts, nieces, or nephews). Since elders have obligations to all children, they discipline not only their own but those in their extended family and even their neighbors as well.

Values which seem to be extolled in this type of interpersonal communication are self-reliance, responsibility, cooperation, diligence, and studiousness. Some behavior patterns which one seems to be cautioned against are deceitfulness, dishonesty, greed, and gossip. Some of the proverbs in this section are given in the contexts in which they may be used.

In *Na tek bod an yu na gyet keej* (Do not take a bird if you do not have a cage), one is advised not to undertake a venture unless adequate preparations are made. Although the symbols of a bird and a cage are used, the proverb refers to man. It is frequently used in reference to young men about to be married who are not sufficiently secure financially to be able to afford a wife.

The proverb *Wen labba tel yu waak, ron laka akarii* (When the *labba* tells one to walk one should run like an *accourie* advises one not to trust an unreliable person. In the proverb the *labba* is used as a symbol for the unreliable person, while the *accourie*, a small rodent which runs very quickly, is used to show how one must react to the unreliable person's advice. The advice given is not merely to run but to do so in a particular manner. If an unreliable person tells one to do something, one must ensure one does the opposite.

The proverb *If krab na waak ii na gyet fat, ii waak tumoch ii a gu a pat* (If the crab does not walk he will not get fat, if he walks too much he will end up in someone's pot) is based on a truism. However, it is applicable both to the crab and to man. The metaphorical meaning behind this proverb is that one must be temperate to avoid disaster.

In *Jakaas eez big ii na heer ii oon stoorii* (The jackasses' ears are big, but he does not hear his own story), one is warned against gossip. In this proverb the jackass is used to symbolize the person who is so foolish that she listens to other people's affairs while neglecting her own. The essence of this proverb is brought out in

3

the situation in which a gossip-monger continually takes bitsand pieces of news from one source to another. This person is always hearing something about someone else. Meanwhile there is a rumor circulating about her, and while others are discussing it, she is apparently unaware of it. The essence of this proverb is brought out in this instance where, "jackasses' ears" are big enough to hear others' affairs but not her own.

This proverb is synonymous to *Yu piip yu matii baksaid yu oon wan a skin oopn* (When you peep your friend's behind, your own will be exposed). This means that in attempting to pry into someone else's affairs, one tends to expose one's self and leave oneself very vulnerable.

The proverb *Pompkin na raip na kot am diip* (If the pumpkin is not ripe do not cut it deeply) advises caution in everything one does. If one wants to cut a pumpkin to see whether it is ripe, one ought not cut it too deeply for the action must result in the loss of the whole pumpkin. One therefore must not act prematurely.

In the lives of many Guyanese the proverb *Haan wash haan mek haan kom kliin* (When one hand washes the other hand both become clean), is much in evidence. People often achieve goals they set for themselves by sharing their resources with others on a cooperative basis. In the Cooperative Republic of Guyana many housing schemes are built on a cooperative basis, in which prospective home owners assist one another in building their homes. In another common practice, the Guyanese pool their money monthly or fortnightly in a "box" to help each other acquire material necessities.

These proverbs dealing with advice when placed contextually demonstrate that although the folk did not have the capacity of explaining their concepts and philosophy in terms of standard language they could do so in terms of the concrete situations available to them. They drew from examples in nature and formulated proverbial sayings to use as a mode of instruction. Proverbs categorized as advice are given in this section. Three versions of each proverb is given:

   a) The creole proverb in phonemic notation.

   b) The literal translation.

   c) The meaning of the proverb in standard language.

1.   a) ***Na put yu hat wee yu haan kyaan riich.***
     b) Do not put your hat where your hand cannot reach.
     c) One must not be overambitious.

2.   a) ***Nyam som tudee, lef som fu tumaroo.***
     b) Eat *(nyam)* some today, leave some for tomorrow.
     c) Always make preparations for the future.

3.   a) ***Yu sii tudee yu na sii tumaroo.***
     b) You have seen today, but you have not seen tomorrow.

c) Make the best of the present, and do not procrastinate.

4.   a) ***Yu kyaan sok keen an wisl.***
   b) You cannot suck cane and whistle.
   c) One shouldn't try to do two things at the same time, for one suffers.

5.   a) ***Yu kyaan gyet tuu swiit outa waan keen nat.***
   b) You cannot get two sweets out of one joint (knot) of cane.
   c) Once you have expended your resources to acquire plea sure in one way, it cannot be used again.

6.   a) ***Paatnaship a liikii ship.***
   b) A partnership is like a leaking ship.
   c) There are a lot of problems in joint ventures.

7.   a) ***A hint from Beniiba mek Kwashiiba tek nootis.***
   b) A hint from Beniba made Kwasiba take notice.
   c) One must seek what one wants.

8.   a) ***Wen yu sii you matii beed a bon wet yu oon.***
   b) When you see your friend's *(matty's)* beard is burning, wet your own.
   c) You must learn from others experience.

9.   a) ***Aal skin tiit na laaf.***
   b) Every act of showing one's teeth (skin-teeth) is not laughter.
   c) Look for the sinister motive in someone's behavior.

10.   a) ***Mek yu bed biifo yu lai dong.***
   b) Make your bed before you lie down.
   c) Make adequate preparations before you undertake a venture.

11.   a) ***Kot yu timba biifo yu haal am.***
   b) Cut your timber before you haul it.
   c) Make adequate preparations before you undertake a venture.

12.   a) ***If nain na noo yu beto aks ten.***
   b) If nine does not know you had better ask ten.
   c) When the desired element is unattainable one must find a substitute.

13.   a) ***Yu piip yu matii baksaid yu oon wan a skin oopn.***
   b) When you peep your friend's backside your own is wide open.
   c) When you mind other people's affairs they mind your own.

14.   a) ***A su mi bai am a su mi sel am.***
   b) It is so I bought it, it is so I am selling it.
   c) Gossip-mongers use this saying to suggest the authenticity of their actions.

15. a) *Wu yu gyet iizii, yu a gu luuz iizii.*
     b) What you get easily, you will lose easily.
     c) People value what they labored to earn.

16. a) *Patwa kom outa trench batam ii se huurii de de biliiv am.*
     b) If the *patwa* comes out of the bottom of the trench and says the *hori* is there, then believe him.
     c) Listen to those in a better position to advise you.

17. a) *Na eeg wa strims na gyet mek ii na big laik weeli.*
     b) It is not the age which the shrimp does not have which causes him not to be big like the whale.
     c) One's ability is not determined by one's age or experience.

18. a) *Jakaas eez big ii na heer ii oon stoorii.*
     b) Although the jackass's ears are big, he does not hear his own story.
     c) People mind other people's business, neglecting their own.

19. a) *Tuu jakass kyan bray waan taim.*
     b) Two jackasses cannot bray at one time.
     c) More is achieved through communication.

20. a) *Di lazii jackaas kyaan kyarii ii oon oots.*
     b) The lazy jackass can't carry his own oats.
     c) Coping with life's problems builds character.

21. a) *Wen karn ii siizn karn-bod riijais, wen di lasiz kom ii kom pon di karn fiil massa.*
     b) When corn is in season the corn bird rejoices; when the losses come they come on the cornfield's master.
     c) A person will rejoice at another's misfortune if he/she stands to gain.

22. a) *Na tek bod an yu na gat keej.*
     b) Do not take a bird when you do not have a cage.
     c) Make adequate preparations before you undertake a venture.

23. a) *Doon main how bod beks, ii kyaan beks wid trii.*
     b) Regardless of how annoyed (vexed) a bird is, he cannot be annoyed (vexed) with a tree.
     c) One should never show ingratitude to one's benefactor.

24. a) *Bush gat eez.*
     b) Bush have ears.
     c) Be wary, for misdeeds committed covertly often surface.

25. a) *Bush gat eez, dutii gat tong.*
     b) Bushes have ears, and the dirt has a tongue.
     c) Secrets or misdeeds committed covertly will eventually surface.

26. a) *Yu kyaan iit yu keek an have it.*
    b) You cannot eat your cake and have it.
    c) Once you have expended your resources to acquire pleasure in one way you cannot use the same resources again.

27. a) *You kyaan gyet om in keek an gyet om in beek.*
    b) You cannot get something in cake and also get it in pancake (bake).
    c) Once you have expended your resources to acquire pleasure in one way you cannot use the same resources again.

28. a) *If yu na gat kongatee a do, yu na ga fo luk fo reen.*
    b) If you do not have *kongatay* at your door, you do not have to look for rain.
    c) If you are innocent you have nothing to worry about.

29. a) *If yu ga kongatee a doo luk out fo reeni.*
    b) If you have *kongatay* at the door look out for rain.
    c) It's a guilty conscience which imputes motives.

30. a) *Haan wash haan mek haan kom kliin.*
    b) When hand washes hand both become clean.
    c) When we assist each other we all prosper.

31. a) *Neva le yu rait haan noo wa yu lef haan a du.*
    b) Never let your right hand know what your left hand is doing.
    c) If you want your secrets to remain secrets keep them from your friends.

32. a) *Dans a batam luk a tap.*
    b) While you are dancing at the bottom you must also be looking at the top.
    c) In everything you do keep a lookout for danger.

33. a) *Wen yu gu a kraab daans, yu mus gyet mud.*
    b) When you go to a crab dance you must get mud.
    c) One who associates with evil companions will be corrupted.

34. a) *If krab na waak ii na gyet fat, ii waak tumoch ii a gu a pat.*
    b) If the crab does not walk it will not get fat, but if it walks too much it may go into the pot.
    c) One should be temperate to avoid disaster.

35. a) *Bat ton ii batii se ii a shit pon maan bot ii a shit pon gaad.*
    b) Bat turns upside down thinking that he is excreting on man, but he is excreting on God.
    c) When you set a trap for someone, another person may fall into it.

36. a) *Bat hang ii batii a tap tink se ii a shit pon gaad.*
    b) Bat hangs upside down thinking that he is excreting on God.
    c) When you set a trap for someone another person may suffer as a result of it.

37. a) *Yu neve mis di waata til di wel run dry.*
b) You never miss the water until the well runs dry.
c) Some things are appreciated only after they are lost.

38. a) *Yu na krass wata, na kus wata muma.*
b) If you haven't crossed the water, do not curse the water—mother.
c) Do not make rash decisions.

39. a) *Aalwaiz trii di wata biifoo yu jump in.*
b) Always try the water before you jump in.
c) Do not undertake rash ventures.

40. a) *Na troo wee dutii wata bifoo yu hav kliin.*
b) Do not throw away dirty water before you have clean water.
c) Treasure what you have even if you desire for something better.

41. a) *Yu kyaan mek blud outa tooni.*
b) You cannot make blood out of stone.
c) The person suffering financial hardship is doing his/her best and cannot do anymore.

42. a) *Blud tika dan wata.*
b) Blood is thicker than water.
c) Relatives support each other.

43. a) *Yu kyaan sen a bai fu duu a maan jab.*
b) You cannot send a boy to do a man's job.
c) An inexperienced person cannot be expected to perform as an experienced one.

44. a) *Fishamaan neva se ii fis stink.*
b) A fisherman never says his fish is stink.
c) One's possessions are always best.

45. a) *Evrii dee a fishin dee but evrii dee na kechin dee.*
b) Every day is fishing day, but every day is not catching day.
c) People who ask favors cannot expect to succeed at all times.

46. a) *Shi moo hoolii dan raichus.*
b) She is more holy than righteous.
c) Appearances are deceptive.

47. a) *Di moo yu wach, di les yu sii.*
b) The more you watch the less you see.
c) People are more secretive when a nosy person is around.

48. a) *A laia wus dan a tiif.*
b) A liar is worse than a thief.
c) Never trust a liar.

49. a) *Shoo mi yu kompanii an ail tel yu huu yuu ar.*
b) Show me your company, and I'll tell you who you are.

c) Your associates are a reflection of your personality.

50. a) *Kom se mi an kom liv wid mi a tuu diffren ting.*
    b) Coming to see me and coming to live with me are two different things.
    c) We can only tell a person's character from close interpersonal interaction.

51. a) *Uman reen neva dun.*
    b) Woman rain is never done.
    c) A nagging woman can be an endless irritant.

52. a) *Gud ridans tu baad rubish.*
    b) Good riddance to bad rubbish.
    c) You are better off without him/her.

53. a) *Emptii bag kyaan stan up.*
    b) An empty bag can't stand up.
    c) A hungry person cannot work effectively.

54. a) *Evrii dee na krismas dee.*
    b) Every day is not Christmas day.
    c) You will not have good fortune all the time.

55. a) *Wen kao mek fight hars no bisniz de.*
    b) When cows are fighting, horses have no business there.
    c) A stranger should not become involved in a family feud.

56. a) *If yu luv de kou yu mus luv di kyaaf.*
    b) If you love the cow you must love the calf.
    c) One should accept the consequences of one's actions.

57. a) *Yu lov de kou, yu na lov de kyaaf.*
    b) You love the cow, but you don't love the calf.
    c) You do not accept the consequences of your actions.

58. a) *Na bai kou if yu kyan gyet frii milk.*
    b) Do not buy a cow if you can get milk freely.
    c) Do not purchase what you can acquire freely.

59. a) *Yu kom fo bai milk na rekn kou.*
    b) If you come to buy milk do not count cows.
    c) Mind your own business.

60. a) *Na lak ov a tong mek kou kyaan taak.*
    b) It's not because the cow has no tongue that she can't talk.
    c) Often one is silent from prudence rather than ignorance.

61. a) *Streenja na noo berin grong.*
    b) A stranger does not know a burial ground.
    c) An outsider doesn't know the pitfalls in a given situation.

62. a) *Bega na chuuza.*
    b) The beggar is not the one who chooses.

c) One who is destitute should accept whatever help is offered.

63. a) *Evrii tub taan pon ii own biihain.*
   b) Every tub must stand on its own behind.
   c) One must strive for self-reliance in life.

64. a) *Belii ful maan tel hungrii belii maa, "kiip haat, budii".*
   b) Full-belly tells hungry-belly to take heart.
   c) It is easy for someone unaffected by a problem to empathize.

65. a) *Spiik wen spookn tu, ansa wen kald.*
   b) Speak when you are spoken to, and answer when you are called.
   c) Do not become involved in altercations that are no concern to you.

66. a) *Howdii and tankii breek noo boonz.*
   b) Howdy and thank you do not break bones.
   c) Common civility will harm no one.

67. a) *Krai-krai piknil neva hav rait.*
   b) A cry-cry child never has rights.
   c) A person who constantly cries "wolf" ceases to be taken seriously.

68. a) *Cuss-cuss neva boor hool in mi kin.*
   b) Curses can't bore a hole in a man's skin.
   c) Mean words do not affect us physically, so ignore them.

69. a) *Kyat fot saaf bot ii a scrach baad.*
   b) Cat foot is soft, but it scratches badly.
   c) Appearances are deceptive.

70. a) *Orinj yeloo bot yu na noo if ii swiit.*
   b) Although the orange may be yellow, you do not know if it is sweet.
   c) One can't judge everything from appearances.

71. a) *Evrii bes fren gat a nex bes fren.*
   b) Every best friend has another best friend.
   c) Guard your secrets well, for as long as they are revealed to one person they are no longer secrets.

72. a) *Wen yu de in bad luk wet paapa self a kot yu.*
   b) When you are suffering from bad luck, wet paper itself could cut you.
   c) A spell of misfortune can cause one's whole outlook to be bleak.

73. a) *Na evrii big heed gat sens.*
   b) Not every big head has sense.
   c) Appearances are deceptive.

74. a) *Laim neva faal far from di trii.*
b) Limes never fall far from the tree.
c) Used derogatorily to insult someone who shows repulsive characteristics of his/her forbearers. It suggests that nothing better was expected of that person.

75. a) *Wen kakrooch gi daans ii neba aks foul.*
b) When cockroach gives a dance, he never asks fowl.
c) One never willingly courts danger.

76. a) *Kakrooch kyaan su drunk ii waak a fowl yaad.*
b) However drunk cockroach may be, he will never walk in fowl's yard.
c) One should discretely avoid those who would harm oneself.

77. a) *Whoo di kyap fit, le ii draw di string.*
b) Who the cap fits let him draw the string.
c) One must accept the consequences of one's actions.

78. a) *Waan taim iz misteek, bot tuu taim iz porpos.*
b) One time is a mistake but two times is on purpose.
c) An unmarried teenager who gets pregnant twice may be ad monished that her behavior is deliberate.

79. a) *Outa di frain pan inta di faia.*
b) Out of the frying pan into the fire.
c) Beware of situations which can lead to more trouble.

80. a) *Teek keer beta dan beg paadn.*
b) Take care is better than beg pardon.
c) Some issues should be avoided.

81. a) *Wa iz na gud fo brekfas na gud fo dina.*
b) What is not good for breakfast is not good for dinner.
c) Do not show favoritism.

82. a) *Na evrii tin kop nak yu a gu.*
b) Not every time a tin cup knocks you are going.
c) Be more selective as to which function you attend.

83. a) *Daag wa yuuz fa sok eeg kyaan lef aaf.*
b) When a dog begins to eat eggs he never stops.
c) Some pleasurable activities once begun are hard to resist.

84. a) *Wen daag a hungrii ii nyam kylabash.*
b) When the dog is hungry he will eat even a calabash.
c) To fill a need one makes do with anything at hand.

85. a) *Daag wid bruk fut fain ii maasta doo.*
b) The dog with a broken foot finds his master's door.
c) There is always a source of help when needed.

11

86. a) *Hungrii daag nyaam roas kaarn.*
    b) A hungry dog will eat roast corn.
    c) One who is in dire straits should utilize what is available to him/her.

87. a) *Yu sii smook, faia de de.*
    b) If you see smoke, fire is there.
    c) Heed warning signs before danger comes.

88. a) *Wa gud fa di guus, gud fo di ganda.*
    b) What is good for the goose is good for the gander.
    c) One deserves to encounter retaliation in kind.

89. a) *Na bai pig in a baag.*
    b) Do not buy a pig in a bag.
    c) Be aware of the value of something before you acquire it.

90. a) *Bai biif yu bai boon; bai lan yu bai rak toon.*
    b) If you buy beef, you buy bone; if you buy land, you also buy rocks or stones.
    c) We should accept the faults as well as the good points of our mates.

91. a) *Blif na gye boon daag na biznis de.*
    b) If the beef does not have bone, the dog has no business there.
    c) A stranger should not be concerned with what is not his/her affair.

92. a) *Wen laba tel yu waak ron laka akarii.*
    b) When labba tells you to walk, run like an accourie.
    c) Never trust a liar.

93. a) *Yu hav fo kriip befo yu waak.*
    b) You have to creep before you walk.
    c) Newly married couples, for example, may be admonished that life moves in stages.

94. a) *Boot in gat batam ii staan near shoor.*
    b) A boat without a bottom stays near to the shore.
    c) Be aware of your shortcomings.

95. a) *Bruk kalabash bring nyew wan.*
    b) A broken calabash brings a new one.
    c) Old trivial things can easily be replaced. This could also be used to mean that borrowers may be forced to buy new items to replace broken ones.

96. a) *Kot yu koat fo suit yu klaat.*
    b) Cut your coat to suit your cloth.
    c) Live within your means.

97. a) *Lil finga se "luk yandah," tum se "luk ya."*

b) Little finger said, "Look yonder"; thumb said, "Look here."
c) When you mind other people's business, they mind yours.

98. a) *If yu finga gat soor na tek um an troo um wee.*
b) If your finger has a sore, do not take it and throw it away.
c) One cannot disown a delinquent member of one's family.

99. a) *Lil fina paint tu big tum an se na gu.*
b) The little finger pointed to the big thumb and said, "Do not go."
c) Leaders are in a position to predict danger and advise accordingly.

100. a) *Ax mi no kweschn an a tel yu no lai.*
b) If you ask me no questions, I will not have to tell you any lies.
c) When you pry into other's affairs, you are likely to receive false information.

101. a) *Wen trobl kech maan ii stan op an stagga; wen trobl kech ooman shi sidong an konsida.*
b) When trouble catches a man he stands up and staggers; when trouble catches a woman she sits down and considers.
c) The sexes handle crises differently.

102. a) *Neva trobl trobl til trobl trobl yuu.*
b) Never trouble trouble until trouble troubles you.
c) Stay clear of problematic issues unless someone implicates you.

103. a) *Nyuu bruum swiip kliin, bot ool wan noo di karna.*
b) New brooms sweep clean, but old ones know the corners.
c) Do not forsake old friends for new because old ones have proven their worth and are more trustworthy.

104. a) *Wen yong foul kak kroo ool kak a gye sens.*
b) When a young rooster (fowl-cock) crows, an old cock will get sense.
c) Standards deteriorate when there is no competition.

105. a) *Evrii fowl fiid pon ii own kraw.*
b) Every fowl feeds on its own craw.
c) Bear your own responsibilities.

106. a) *Evrii taim foul drink waata, ii hais ii hed a tap an se tank gaad*
b) Every time the fowl drinks water, he holds his head upright and says, "Thank God."
c) Always give thanks for your blessings.

107. a) *Kontree briiz a mek kroo an iiglii lait on waan lain.*
b) Contrary breeze makes the crow and the eagle alight on the same line.

c) In the event of a crisis, social barriers are likely to be ignored.

108. a) *Makaw ask parot if mangoo raip, ii se waan, waan.*
b) When the macaw asked the parrot if the mangoes were ripe, he said, "One, one."
c) Do not divulge everything, leave some things for others to discover for themselves.

109. a) *Tortl na waant trobl mek ii waak wid ii hous pon ii bak.*
b) It is because the turtle does not want trouble that he walks with his house on his back.
c) One should always be prepared for any eventuality.

110. a) *Maan laik kow shit, drai on tap an haad at di batam.*
b) Men are like cow shit, dry on top and hard on the bottom.
c) Men are deceptive.

111. a) *Na tek neks maan ai an sii.*
b) Do not take another man's eye and see.
c) Do not accept everything other people say without verifying it.

112. a) *Wen maan mek iiself suga ii matii a sok am.*
b) When a man makes himself sugar, his friends will suck him.
c) Do not allow friends and associates to abuse your good nature.

113. a) *Wen maan don suk keen ii dash piiling a groun.*
b) When a man is finished (done) sucking cane, he dashes the peeling on the ground.
c) Often what you do not need is carelessly discarded.

114. a) *If yu ai na sii yu mout na fu taak.*
b) If your eyes did not see, your mouth is not to talk (repeat).
c) Beware of heresy.

115. a) *Yu ai biga dan yu belii.*
b) Your eyes are bigger than your stomach (belly).
c) Cease to act in a greedy manner.

116. a) *Wem muma ded famlii don.*
b) When the mother is dead, the family is finished (done).
c) Since mothers keep the family together, when a mother dies the family bond is broken.

117. a) *Yu na ga muma yu ga fo sok graanii.*
b) If you do not have a mother, you have to suckle your grandmother.
c) You must make the best of what you have.

118. a) *Di moo yu liv di moo yu laarn.*
b) The more you live the more you learn.
c) Experience teaches wisdom.

119. a) *If yu na live a hous yu na noo wee ii a liik.*
    b) If you do not live at a house, you do not know where it is leaking.
    c) You can never assess a situation from a few casual encounters.

120. a) *Duu gud an gud wil fala yu.*
    b) Do good and good will follow you.
    c) We will be rewarded for our good deeds.

121. a) *Wok moo taak les.*
    b) Work more, talk less.
    c) Work, not idle chatter, is rewarded.

122. a) *If yu doan weer di shooz yu doon noo wa ii a pinch.*
    b) If you don't wear the shoes; you don't know where they pinch.
    c) Only those intimately aware of the circumstances can identify with it.

123. a) *Tong na ga tiit bot ii a bait fu truu.*
    b) The tongue does not have teeth, yet it bites.
    c) Gossip can hurt even though it is not physical.

124. a) *Na evriiting skala noo ii larn from tiicha.*
    b) Not everything that a scholar knows he learned from a teacher.
    c) There are many modes of learning in life.

125. a) *Na aal whuu gu a chorch hous a gu fo pree.*
    b) Not everyone who goes to church goes to pray.
    c) Don't take everything at face value.

126. a) *Doan bait aaf moo dan yu kyan chuu.*
    b) Do not bite off more than you can chew
    c) Take time to achieve the best results.

127. a) *Na kyast perlz biifoor swain.*
    b) Do not cast pearls before swine.
    c) Do not give someone gifts they will not appreciate.

128. a) *If ail a floaat waata de a batam.*
    b) If oil is floating water is at the bottom.
    c) Sometimes a little evidence can betray one.

129. a) *Yu kyaan drink beer an belch mabii.*
    b) You cannot drink beer and belch *mauby.*
    c) What you sow, is that which you will reap.

130. a) *Yu kyaan chew boon wid gum.*
    b) You cannot chew bones with your gum.
    c) Expertise is needed to achieve success in many endeavors.

131. a) *Wen tuu big batl de a teebl lil wan na bisniz de.*

b) When two big bottles are on the table, the little one has no business there.

c) Know your place when you are among superiors.

132. a) *If yu plaant plaantin yu kyaan riip kasava.*

b) If you plant plantains you cannot reap cassava.

c) Whatever you sow, it is that which you will reap.

133. a) *Aal kasava gat seem skin bot aal na teest seem wee.*

b) All cassava has the same skin, but all doesn't taste the same way.

c) People have different personalities.

134. a) *Big trii faal dong goot bait ii liif.*

b) When a big tree falls down, the goat bites the leaves.

c) Once authority is impotent, subordinates abuse privileges.

135. a) *Oonlii naif a noo wa in pumpkin belii.*

b) Only the knife knows what is in the pumpkin's belly.

c) We can only tell a person's faults from close interpersonal interaction.

136. a) *Pomkin na raip na kot am diip.*

b) If the pumpkin is not ripe, do not cut it deeply.

c) Do not act prematurely.

137. a) *Wen koknut faal from trii ii kyaan fasn bak.*

b) When a coconut falls from the tree, it cannot be reattached.

c) Some things cannot be reversed.

138. a) *Monii don, fren don.*

b) When money is finished, so is friendship.

c) When one's money is spent, love is over.

139. a) *Tink fos biifoor yu taak.*

b) Always think first before you offer an opinion (talk).

c) Do not make rash decisions.

140. a) *Neva gu a stoor a nait a buy blak klaat.*

b) Never go to the store in the night to buy black cloth.

c) Some ventures must only be undertaken when all aspects are favorable.

141. a) *Dutii powda noobadii want am.*

b) Dirty powder, nobody wants it.

c) One with a disreputable past is not respected.

142. a) *Tu much sidong a bruk trousiz.*

b) Too much sitting down breaks one's trousers.

c) Lazy people wear out their pants and get nothing done.

143. a) *Klaat iisii fu dutii bot haad fu waash.*

b) Cloth is easily dirtied, but it is hard to clean.

c) A reputable reputation once blemished is difficult to regain.

144. a) *Evrii roop gat tuu endz.*
    b) Every rope has two ends.
    c) Be open to other possibilities.

145. a) *If dutii ah de a roof tap yu baril ah kech am.*
    b) If dirt is on your roof, your (water) barrel will catch it.
    c) You may be unconsciously exposing those around you to undesirable traits.

146. a) *Di luks a di pudin iz na di teest.*
    b) The looks of the pudding is not the taste.
    c) Do not judge things by appearances.

Warning

Parents often have cause to speak out in an angry or displeased manner when rebuking a child or to voice disapproval for their child's behavior. For this reason, the proverbs in this category may be used by parents to chide or scold their children. They incorporate a measure of caution and are meant to reproach in a mild and constructive manner. Some of the proverbs in this section are given in the contexts in which they may be used.

The maxim *muun a ron til dee keech am* (The moon runs until the day catches it) warns one not to take chances for one day one will be caught. The meaning is evidenced in the following context. A certain unemployed lad took to stealing cycles and selling them for a living. Many people suspected him of being involved in illegal activities, and some of them confided their fears to his parents. When questioned, the young man denied being involved in any unlawful matter. Some time afterward, the parents were informed that their son was seen removing a bicycle from outside a movie theater. When confronted with this information, the young man again denied being involved in any such misconduct. The father warned his son that *muun a ron til dee kech am*. One day a policeman locked his bicycle outside a cinema and went into a show. After half an hour, he left as the show was unsatisfactory. Outside he saw a lad trying to open his cycle. He approached him and asked whether he was having a problem. The lad replied that he was having difficulty opening his cycle as he seemed to have misplaced the key for it. On hearing this, the officer apprehended the youth, took him to the nearest police station, and had a charge instituted against him.

In the same way as the moon keeps on its usual course from hour to hour until day breaks, in the same way the lad kept committing the very offense until he was caught. The reflection of society one gets from this situation is that in life you can take chances committing illegal activities, but one day you will be caught.

In the proverb *If yu plee wid di pupii, yu goo gyet bit wid di fliiz* (If you play with the puppy, you will be bitten by the fleas), one is warned against associating with undesirables. The proverb stresses that one must choose one's friends wisely, for if one keeps company with shady characters, one will be influenced to act in like manner. Even the innocent who associate with disreputable characters is likely to be corrupted.

Sexual connotation is implicit in *Klaim papaw trii an ii beer fu yu* (If you climb a papaw tree it will bear for you). The connotation is that one must expect to suffer the consequences for sexual misdeeds. The proverb warns young people that pregnancy may result from illicit sexual activities or one might even catch a sexually transmitted disease.

Keeping realistic goals is evident in *Bod flai tuu hai mus pas ii nes* (Birds that fly too high must pass their nest). This proverb warns that one who exceeds one's limitations is likely to fall beyond recovery. One, therefore, should not elevate one's self above one's station but keep one's expectations in perspective.

Proverbs categorized as warnings are given in this section.

1. a) *Pors ful, plentii fren.*
   b) One whose purse is full has plenty of friends.
   c) Beware of opportunists.

2. a) *Yu kyan kyari haas a di wata but yu kyaan mek im drink.*
   b) You can carry a horse to the water, but you cannot make him/her drink.
   c) A stubborn person can ruin the best laid plans.

3. a) *If win na bloo liif na sheek.*
   b) If the wind did not blow, the leaf would not have shaken.
   c) Gossip-mongers deserve what they get.

4. a) *Na kot aaf yu nooz fo spail yu fees.*
   b) Do not cut off your nose to spoil your face.
   c) Do not court danger.

5. a) *Bod flai tuu hai mus pas ii nes.*
   b) Birds that fly too high must pass their nests.
   c) Keep realistic goals.

6. a) *A haas gud haart mek maan raid am as ii laik.*
   b) It is the horse's good heart (nature) that makes man ride him as he likes.
   c) Advantage is taken of the willing person.

7. a) *Whoo di kyap fit, le ii weer it.*
   b) Who the cap fits let him wear it.
   c) One must accept the consequences of one's actions.

8. a) *Plee wid mongkii but na plee wid ii teel.*
   b) You may play with the monkey, but do not play with his tail.
   c. This warns an intrusive person not to overstep one's bounds.

9. a) *Moo mongkii klaim moo ii shoo ii teel.*
   b) The higher the monkey climbs, the more he exposes himself.
   c) Take reproof humbly when you have committed a fault or you will only make matters worse.

10. a) *If yu plee wid di pupii, yu goo gyet bit wid di fliiz.*
    b) If you play with the puppy, you will be bitten by the fleas.
    c) You will reap the consequences of your actions.

11. a) *Fala patn neba out a trobl.*
    b) A person who imitates (follows others blindly) is never out of trouble.
    c) Beware of your associates.

12. a) *Gi yu an inch yu tek a yaad.*
    b) If I give you an inch do not take a yard.

c) Don't abuse your privileges.

13. a) ***A gud fren iz betah dan monii in di pakit.***
    b) A good friend is better than money in the pocket.
    c) Good friends can be indispensable.

14. a) ***Sorii fu maaga daag, maaga daag tun roun bait yu.***
    b) When you are sorry for a meager dog, the meager dog will turn around and bite you.
    c) Kindness is often repaid with ingratitude.

15. a) ***Maan gat tumuch tong ii pee ii daadii det.***
    b) If a man has too much tongue, he will pay his father's debts.
    c) Don't expose family affairs.

16. a) ***Wen maan kyaan daans ii se muzik na gud.***
    b) When a man cannot dance, he says the music is no good.
    c) People usually blame others for their shortcomings.

17. a) ***Du fu du na oobiiah.***
    b) Doing to someone what they did to you is not evil (obeah).
    c) Evil is often reciprocated for evil.

18. a) ***Horii horii mek baad korii.***
    b) Excessive hurrying (hurry-hurry) makes bad curry.
    c) One should take time if one wants the best results.

19. a) ***Plee plee a bring nee nee.***
    b) Excessive play (play-play) brings crying.
    c) What starts off as a joke may have serious repercussions.

20. a) ***A daag wa a bring boon a kyarii boon.***
    b) The dog which brings bones carries bones.
    c) People who bring news (gossip) will take news.

21. a) ***Kyat na de rat tek oovo.***
    b) When the cat is not there, the rat will take over.
    c) Once authority is absent, subordinates do what they please.

22. a) ***Wa iz plee fo lil bai iz ded fo krapoo.***
    b) What is play for a little boy is death for the crapaud.
    c) What is amusement for one may be harmful for another.

23. a) ***Pig aks ii muma wa mek yu mout su lang; muma se, weet yu a groo yu a gu miit am.***
    b) The pig asked its mother, "What makes your mouth so long?" The mother said, "Wait, you are growing; you will meet it."
    c) One should not laugh at another's misfortune because it is possible that one suffers in the same way.

24. a) ***Hag aks ii muma wa mek shi mout sa lang, shi se, tek taim piknii yu go miit am.***
    b) The hog asked his mother, "What makes your mouth so long?" She replied, "Take time my child; you will meet it."

c) One is advised not to laugh at another person's misfortune because it is possible that one suffers in the same way.

25. a) ***A seem stik wa lik taam a lik dik.***
    b) That same stick which whips (licks) Tom will be used to whip (lick) Dick.
    c) We are all subjected to the same treatment.

26. a) ***Trobl de a poola wata bring am dong.***
    b) When trouble is at the poulder, the water will bring it down.
    c) We cannot feel free from something because we are far away.

27. a) ***Maan na laik yu ii gi yu baskit fo fech wata.***
    b) When a man does not like you, he will give you a basket to carry (fetch) water.
    c) One's enemies give one impossible tasks to perform.

28. a) ***Reen a faal bokit na ful dyuu kyaan ful am.***
    b) Since the rain fell and the bucket was not filled, then the dew cannot fill it.
    c) If greater efforts did not achieve results, lesser would not.

29. a) ***Muun a ron til dee kech am.***
    b) The moon runs until the day catches it.
    c) You can take chances, but one day you will be caught.

30. a) ***Klaim papaw trii an ii beer fu yu.***
    b) If you climb a papaw tree it will bear for you.
    c) You will reap the consequences of your actions.

31. a) ***Unwilin piknii doz dutii smaal.***
    b) An unwilling child defecates small.
    c) Laziness leads to poverty rather than prosperity.

32. a) ***Di mo yu wach di les yu sii.***
    b) The more you watch the less you will see.
    c) Used in reference to snoopy individuals to warn that they will not gain more information by prying.

33. a) ***Wen ai taak, no daagz baak.***
    b) When I talk let no dogs bark.
    c) Do not question my authority.

34. a) ***Piknii wa na heer mooma ii a fiil.***
    b) The child (pickney) who does not hear his mother will feel.
    c) The disobedient child will meet with misfortune.

Threat

The proverbs in this category are used as a means of self-preservation. They are confrontational and are used to an aggressor whom one hopes to get even with at some time. They may also be viewed as tools for conflict resolution. If one is in an argument with another and losing control, an apt proverb may be "thrown in an opponent's face," or used as a defense mechanism, to bolster self-esteem or to settle scores. Many Guyanese believe that when one wrongs someone else they, "will reap what they sow."

Hence in a confrontation the injured person who harbors bitterness or suffers from a wrong will use one of these proverbs to signal that the injured party will be pursuing a vendetta against the enemy. They are used "as consolation for impotence, the weapon of the weak against the provocation of the strong. In an argument, an apt proverb will often win conviction. As a veiled threat it carries the efficacy of a curse."[1] Some of the proverbs in this section are given in the contexts in which they may be used.

An injured party out for revenge may tell an opponent taim *laanga dan twain* (Time is longer than twine). This concise maxim reminds the listener that time's infinity allows an offended person adequate scope for avenging himself. One, therefore, must be careful what one does as given enough time one will reap the consequences. This maxim conveys the message that one who is carrying a vendetta need not seek revenge in kind but can retaliate in various ways. The offender should always be on guard as the wronged person can seek revenge at any time.

Often *Liif faal a wata ii na ratn seem taim* (A leaf falls into the water, but it does not rot immediately). This proverb may be used as a threat against someone who tries to take advantage of another's misfortune. It implies that the unfortunate one, like the leaf in the water, is not yet entirely useless or helpless and can therefore get even with the enemy.

A female rival may hurl the proverb *Di hool yu dig fu mii yu gyan faal in am* (The hole that you dig for me you will fall into it) at an adversary. Very often two females will get into a dispute because they are rivals for the same male. When insults begin to fly, this proverb may be thrown as a threat to maim the adversary. If the female believes that the other woman is working evil or obeah against her, she may threaten that her evil will turn against her.

In this proverb *Ool granii swear fu kyatapila, kyatapila swear fo wok shi belii* (While the old lady is swearing for the caterpillar, the caterpillar is swearing to act as a laxative [to work her belly]). The caterpillar *calalu*, a type of spinach, is an edible weed, overconsumption of which acts as a laxative. When thrown at an adversary, this proverb indicates that while one is plotting to harm another, one's enemy is also hatching his/her own plots.

Proverbs categorized as threats are given in this section:

1. a) ***Di hool yu dig fu mii yu gyan faal in am.***
    b) The hole you dig for me you will fall into it.
    c) Your evil will turn against you.

2. a) ***Whoo laaf laas laaf di bes.***
    b) Who laughs last will laugh the best.
    c) Used as a threat to someone who has wronged another. It suggests that no wrongdoing goes unpunished.

3. a) ***Smaat flai lak op in kou aas.***
    b) The smart fly is locked up in the cow's ass.
    c) Your cunning attitude will lead to your downfall.

4. a) ***Aliigeeta tel sonfish awii gu miit a staap-aaf.***
    b) Alligator told sunfish, "We will meet at the stop-off."
    c) One will get even with one's enemy when he/she is cornered.

5. a) ***Wo swiitn goot mout doz hot ii belii.***
    b) What sweetens the goat's mouth will hurt his belly.
    c) You will suffer from the effects of your wrongdoing.

6. a) ***Wa kom aaf a hed a drap a shoolda.***
    b) What comes off of the head drops onto the shoulder.
    c) You will feel the effects of your actions.

7. a) ***Waan dee waan dee yu hed a gu fasn a samon kop.***
    b) One day your head will become stuck (fastened) in a salmon cup.
    c) You will feel the effects of your wrong deeds sometime.

8. a) ***Fus laaf in di ending.***
    b) First laugh is not the ending.
    c) Given time, one can get even with an enemy.

9. a) ***Bukit a gu a wel evrii dee waan dee ii batam gu drap.***
    b) If a bucket goes to the well every day, one day its bottom will drop out.
    c) Those who habitually engage in wrongdoing will eventually be apprehended and be made to pay the consequences.

10. a) ***Tudee fu mii tumarrau fu yuu.***
    b) Today for me tomorrow for you.
    c) Used as a threat to someone who has wronged another. It suggests that no wrongdoing ever goes unpunished.

11. a) ***Evrii daag gat ii dee.***
    b) Every dog has his day.
    c) My time will come.

12. a) ***Taim laanga dan twain.***
    b) Time is longer than twine.

c) Given enough time you will reap the consequences of your misdeeds.

13. a) *Na matta how pumpkin vain run ii mus drai up wan dee.*
    b) It doesn't matter how a pumpkin vine runs; it will dry up one day.
    c) You will eventually get what you deserve.

14. a) *Dee gat nuf wais fu hang daag widout putin strin rung ii nek.*
    b) There are many ways of hanging a dog without putting a string around its neck.
    c) Revenge can be achieved in several ways.

15. a) *A fas mek anansi de a hous tap.*
    b) It is fastness (inquisitiveness) which caused Anansi to live in the rafters.
    c) One who meddles might be forced into seclusion for his/her own safety.

16. a) *Ool granii swear fu kyatapila, kyatapila swear fo wok shi belii.*
    b) Old granny swears to eat the caterpillar, (a type of wild spinach). The caterpillar swears (pledges) to act as a laxative (to work her belly).
    c) If you trouble me I will retaliate.

17. a) *Everii dee yu strait dangkii, waan dee ii go kik yu.*
    b) Every day you strike donkey, one day he will kick you.
    c) The oppressed will rebel.

18. a) *Liif faal a wata ii na ratn seem taim.*
    b) When a leaf falls into the water, it does not rotten at the same time.
    c) Be on your guard for I will avenge myself at some time.

19. a) *Spit a di skii ii su faal a yu fais.*
    b) Spit up to the sky, and it will fall in your face.
    c) Resentment shown toward others will backfire on you.

20. a) *Yu kyan ron bot yu kyaan haid.*
    b) You can run but you cannot hide.
    c) You will suffer eventually.

Encouragement

Some proverbs seem to be a source of encouragement. Life never runs smoothly, and proverbs serve the purpose of instilling hope and confidence and encouraging one to be courageous when confronted with adversity. These may be used to placate a disappointed person experiencing a sense of hopelessness. These also serve to inspire one to work harder in the face of disappointment, to gird oneself to face the inevitable, and to encourage relentless perseverance in striving to achieve one's goals. These are motivational expressions to keep one going in the face of physical or emotional agony or disaster. More often the proverb is told to one by someone else; however, other users talk to themselves by means of proverbs.

A number of proverbs in this section seem to function as "mottos or inspirational phrases"[1] that informants rely upon to help them to persevere at particular tasks, to reach certain levels of achievement, or otherwise to help them feel more at ease. In effect, speakers apply the proverbs to themselves in internal dialogues or "idionarration," a significantly different use of proverbs than is customarily discussed. This type of proverb is "important in inner discourse and carries significant meaning, within the privacy of the psyche."[2] Some of the proverbs in this section are given in the contexts in which they may be used.

This proverb *Byuugl gat poua wen raiat staat* (The bugle has power when the riot starts), probably arose during slavery. The bugle usually lay idle until a slave had gotten away or a riot had started, at which time it was blown to alert the security forces to their positions. Based on this situation the slaves formulated this proverb. The reflections one gets from this is that even the lowly, despised, and apparently useless may be energized or motivated when the time is opportune.

Sexual symbolism is evident in *Yu kyaan gyet om az a rees hars yu gon gyet om az a kyab hars* (If you cannot get it as a racehorse, you will get it as a cab horse). This proverb is frequently used by men in reference to some women who might think the men are their social inferiors and too lowly to date. When a man perhaps tries to get this beautiful young woman to go out with him and she refuses, he uses this proverb. The consideration in the proverb is that when the woman in question has suffered some disillusionment and lost her pride she may agree to be friendly toward the man in question. Racehorses are very difficult to obtain, but cab horses are numerous.

Women who suffer a miscarriage are frequently consoled with *Jog faal dong wata troo we ii na brok* (The jug fell down and the water was thrown away, but the jug was not broken). This proverb is frequently used to encourage someone not to be disheartened for all is not lost. It could be used in regard to a woman who suffered a miscarriage as a means of assuring her that although an opportunity may be lost, there is still hope for obtaining the desired child in the future.

Perseverance may lead to success for those who believe that *Waak fu notng beta dan sidong fu notng* (To walk for nothing is better than to sit down for nothing). In times of economic woes when downsizing seems to be the order of the day, causing many to lose their jobs, one very easily becomes despondent and does not feel inclined to go job hunting for fear of rejection. However, going to more interviews even after being rejected is better than staying at home under the pretext that one would not get the job after all. This proverb may be used as a source of encouragement to suggest that, since one has nothing to lose and everything to gain, perseverance may eventually lead to success.

Proverbs categorized as encouragement are given in this section.

1. a) **Byuugl gat poua wen raiat staat.**
   b) The bugle has power when the riot starts.
   c) Everything has its own importance at given times.

2. a) **Yu kyaan gyet om az a rees hars yu gon gyet om az a kyab hars.**
   b) If you can't get it as a racehorse, you will get it as a cab horse.
   c) Something which is unattainable when perfect may be at tainable when faulty.

3. a) **Yu mek yu bed haad yu lie on it haad; yu mek yu bed saaf yu lie on it saaf.**
   b) If you make your bed hard, you will lie on it hard. If you make your bed soft, you will lie on it soft.
   c) Take control, as your circumstances depend on you.

4. a) **Waan dee waan dee kongatee.**
   b) One day, one day *kongatay.*
   c) Persevere and success will come sometime. Could also be used as a threat to indicate that one will get even sometime.

5. a) **Di langes roop gat a end.**
   b) The longest rope has an end.
   c) Bear up, as nothing lasts forever. Could also be used as a threat to mean that the person wronged will get even some time.

6. a) **Jog faal dong wata troo we ii na brok.**
   b) The jug fell down and the water was thrown away, but the jug did not break.
   c) One must not be disheartened by one's misfortune.

7. a) **Na evrii kou wa krai ii want wata fo drink.**
   b) Not every cow which cries wants water to drink.
   c) Things are not always what they seem.

8. a) **Na aal daag wa a bark a bait.**

b) Not every dog which barks bites.

c) Some things are only seemingly difficult.

9. a) ***Yu doon noo gud maninija til iisteet brok dong.***
    b) You do not know a good manager till the estate breaks down.
    c) One only misses a good thing when it has gone.

10. a) ***Yu kyaan blak, oglii an stupid.***
    b) You cannot be black, ugly, and stupid.
    c) Everything cannot be against you at the same time.

11. a) ***We ginii bod a hala na de ii a lee.***
    b) Where the guinea bird is crying he is not laying there.
    c) Appearances are often deceptive.

12. a) ***Waak fu notng beta dan sidong fu notng.***
    b) To walk for nothing is better than to sit down for nothing.
    c) Those who persevere may eventually succeed.

13. a) ***Waan waan dutii bil daam.***
    b) One, one dutty will build a dam.
    c) Everything takes time, so being frugal will pay off.

14. a) ***Lil ax kyan kot dong big trii.***
    b) A little ax can cut down a big tree.
    c) Some things that appear insurmountable can be achieved by perseverance.

15. a) ***No peen no gain.***
    b) No pain, no gain.
    c) Success is achieved through hard work.

16. a) ***Lil pepa bun hat.***
    b) A little bit of pepper burns hot.
    c) Appearances are often deceptive.

17. a) ***Lil waata kyan out big faia.***
    b) A little water can put out a big fire.
    c) Some seemingly impossible things can be surmounted.

18. a) ***Wen waan door shut, anuda waan oopn.***
    b) When one door is closed, another opens.
    c) There is always hope for achieving your goals.

19. a) ***Lil bai na klaim lada tu tun big maan.***
    b) A little boy does not climb a ladder to become a big man.
    c) One can only mature with time.

20. a) ***Na waan taim a faia mek peez a bwail.***
    b) It is not one time on the fire which causes peas to boil.
    c) Some things are only achieved with time.

21. a) ***Na evrii krab hool gat drab.***
    b) Not every crab hole has crabs.
    c) Some things may not turn out to be the way you expected.

22. a) *Tortl kyaan waak if ii na put ii hed outa ii shel.*
    b) The turtle cannot walk if he does not put his head out of his shell.
    c) You may need to take risks to achieve your desires.

23. a) *Fish a de a wata bot na a daam tap.*
    b) The fish lives in the water, not on the top of the dam.
    c) One does not have to be knowledgeable in every situation.

24. a) *Reen a faal a rof yu put bukit a kach am.*
    b) When it is raining onto the roof, put a barrel to catch it.
    c) Grasp opportunities as they arise.

25. a) *Evrii bush a man a nait taim.*
    b) Every bush is a man at night.
    c) Things seem worse than they really are when we are afraid.

26. a) *Sloo faia a bwail haad kowheel.*
    b) A slow fire boils hard cow heel.
    c) If one perseveres, one can make great accomplishments.

27. a) *Dutii waata kyan put out faia.*
    b) Dirty water can put out a fire.
    c) Do not give up hope, for a seemingly useless person can eventually make good.

28. a) *Haan gu, haan kom.*
    b) When one hand goes, another hand comes.
    c) There is always a source of comfort.

29. a) *Afta kloud, kleer skai.*
    b) After clouds comes a clear sky.
    c) Your problems are only temporary.

30. a) *Deer iz a bend in evrii riva.*
    b) There is a bend in every river.
    c) Thre is always a turning point in life.

31. a) *Big trii na kot dong wid waan bloo.*
    b) A big tree is not cut down with one blow.
    c) Halfhearted attempts will not lead to success.

Indifference

The proverbs in this section seem to reflect indifference to some situations. Perhaps this is a universal viewpoint based on the practice of not interfering in what is not one's business; for example, domestic altercations or family squabbles. This type of proverb seems to be suggesting that one is to be impartial or neutral to a situation and seems to be stressing qualities of aloofness, detachment, disinterest, or lack of enthusiasm. Perhaps in life some situations might indeed be beyond our control and therefore should be accepted for what they are.

Some of the proverbs in this section are given in the contexts in which they may be used.

In *massa bul; massa kou* (The master's bull; the master's cow), one seems to be cautioned about interfering in domestic altercations. The following dialogue exemplifies this.

JUDGE: Ramsingh, did you visit Henry on the twentieth of February last?
RAMSINGH: Yes, your worship.
JUDGE: Tell the court what you saw.
RAMSINGH: Me see Henry take a cutlass and chap (cut) up he wife.
JUDGE: What did you do?
RAMSINGH: Nothing, sir.
JUDGE: Why didn't you intervene?
RAMSINGH: Me a stranger, sir. Massa bul; massa kou.

This proverb must have come into existence during slavery or "massa day." It is used to bring out the meaning that one should not concern one's self with what is not one's affair. The proverb illustrated reflects on similar occurrences in the Guyana society which abounds with controversial male/female relationships and the incidents which result from them.

The maxim *Blakman belii bakra mout* (The blackman's belly, the white man's mouth) seems to suggest that while the stomach is important to the "blackman" the mouth is important to the "white." It depends on the assumption that African- Guyanese people in Guyana are not satisfied unless their stomachs are filled while the European- Guyanese is content with a tasty morsel. This proverb reflects on the social and economic conditions of the society. Because of his large appetite and relatively poor economic position, the African-Guyanese is concerned with quantity rather than quality, with which the economically superior European- Guyanese is concerned.

A person with a prison record may bolster his self-esteem with *Jeel in mek fu daag* (Jail was not made for dogs). This maxim is often used as a defense mechanism in response to people who reproach others for having been to prison. It argues that if men did not commit misdeeds and have cause to be incarcerated there would be no need for prisons. It is frequently put forward by a person as a show of bravado when, indeed, the person is ashamed of having spent time in prison.

In *Mi navel string berii hee* (My navel string is buried here), one tries to assert one's rights. Someone who is challenged for returning to one's community after living away from it may use this proverb to suggest indifference to others' negativism and one's unquestionable right to live there. In rural Guyana some still follow the custom in which the umbilical cord (navel string) is buried under a fruit-bearing tree. This symbolizes that the child has a permanent claim to the community in which he was born.

A recent North American incident aptly portrays the proverb *Tiif from tiif mek gad laaf* (Stealing from a thief makes God laugh). A certain felon called the superior court judge to say that he would be unable to attend his scheduled sentencing for car theft because his own car had been stolen. He was the victim of his own crime. This is a classic case of "thief from thief."

Proverbs categorized as indifference are given in this section.

1. a) **Massa bul; massa kou.**
    b) The master's bull; the master's cow.
    c) A stranger should not become involved in family affairs.

2. a) **Blakman belii bakra mout.**
    b) The stomach is important to the blackman, the mouth is to the white man.
    c) Social position may influence what we regard as important.

3. a) **Massa haas; massa graas.**
    b) The master's horse; the master's grass.
    c) One is free to treat one's possessions in any manner one pleases.

4. a) **Famlii kotlish na a kot diip.**
    b) One's family's cutlass does not cut deeply.
    c) Family disputes are quickly settled.

5. a) **Taim fo muul taim fo lang cheen.**
    b) When it is time for the mule, it is time for the long chain.
    c) Some things complement each other.

6. a) **Tiif from tiif mek gad laaf.**
    b) Stealing from a thief makes God laugh.
    c) It is gratifying to see someone suffer the way he/she made you suffer.

7. a) **Yu kyaan fiid kriiool pon fufu.**
    b) You cannot feed Creoles on *fufu*.
    c) Creole people love a lot of food.

8. a) **Sin a beer blasom**
    b) Sin bears blossom.
    c) Evil perpetuates evil.

9. a) ***Dem laik batii an poozii.***
   b) They are like one's buttocks *(battie)* and a potty *(posie)*.
   c) They are inseparable.

10. a) ***Evrii kou fo ii kyaaf.***
    b) Every cow will be there for his calf.
    c) One is expected to support one's own.

11. a) ***Jeel in mek fu daag.***
    b) The jail was not made for dogs.
    c) Prison is not so bad after all, as it was made for man.

12. a) ***Nyuu maninja nyuu ruul***
    b) A new manager will make new rules.
    c) Every boss makes his own laws.

13. a) ***No beta di baril no beta de herin.***
    b) No better the barrel, no better the herring.
    c) Children take after their parents.

14. a) ***Blud fala veen.***
    b) Blood follows the veins.
    c) Children exhibit similar traits to their parents.

15. a) ***Maan strenth de a ii haan wuman strenth de a shii mout.***
    b) A man's strength lies in his hand; a woman's strength lies in her mouth.
    c) Men resort to violence; women resort to loquacity.

16. a) ***Mi navel string berii hee.***
    b) My navel string is buried here.
    c) I have an unbreakable bond to this community.

Criticism

Sociology may be defined as, "the theory of social positions, relationships and groups."[1] This theory involves tasks of a formal, historical, and interpretive nature. The formal analysis would deal with matters relating to types of human and group relationships and the processes and conditions which give rise to the origin, the maintenance, the change, and the dissolution of these relationships and groups. The historical analysis deals with the evolution of typical relationships and groups, of their role and function in different concrete situations and historical settings, and of the ways in which these conditions may be influenced by other aspects of social life— religion, economic, political, and cultural.

Sociology can then be said to be concerned with the way of life of a people. It relates to types of human and group relationships and conditions which give rise to the origin, the maintenance, and the dissolution of these relationships. Guyanese creole proverbs give insights into the ways and behavior of the Guyanese people. They apply not only to the social but also to the economic, political, and cultural conditions. They tell of relationships between rich and poor people and can apply to rich and poor nations as well. In assessing a situation and passing judgment upon it, this type of proverb holds up a mirror image in the hope that the individuals referred to will monitor their behavior so that it does not fall outside of the accepted norms of the social group.

In being critical, proverbs are meant to make one think carefully about social relationships, reassess one's conduct, and seek to conform with accepted societal patterns. They serve to reveal certain attitudes important in social life and to remind one to weigh carefully all the possible consequences of one's actions. Often they leave one perplexed to ponder and think seriously to fathom the meaning of the proverbs. Some of the proverbs in this section are given in the contexts in which they may be used.

The maxim *If yu fain a goo brooch a dans haal a dans haal yu gu laas am* (If you find a gold broach in the dance hall you will lose it there) implies that if something is gotten easily it will not be valued. It is applicable to "pork-knockers" who make rich claims but squander their money soon after they have gotten it. For example, the story is often told of a "pork-knocker" who had just returned from Guyana's hinterland and was walking along the road when he dropped a dollar. He immediately scratched a match and lit a twenty-dollar bill to look for the dollar. Others are said to have bought out entire spirit shops when they struck it rich in the gold mines. If one looks at this proverb in the context of the life of a "pork-knocker," one realizes that he is in self-exile from society. When he goes to seek his fortune he hardly ever returns to the society from which he came. This proverb reflects the idea that when the "pork-knocker" becomes wealthy he needs to assert himself even if only for a short while.

Absence of a positive movement leaves a situation open to abuse. This meaning is evident in *Ashij kool daag lai dong* (Ashes cold, dog lie down). An ASCRIA[2] (African Society for Cultural Relations with Independent Africa) bulletin (1968) in speaking about development in Guyana once said,

> A nationalist policy at home, a Caribbean policy, and Afro-Asian companionship have been attempted but these policies have been weakened by the cultural non-commitment of our society. We have failed to develop a cultural movement. Because of this we have been left prey to the cultural aggression of the North Atlantic, an essentially European power center. The absence of a positive movement in culture has left us open to the assault of the juke box, the radio, the cinema, the missionary. As these become more active on traditional lines the scope of our independence is reduced. We lose our creative power, we develop mimic personalities, not based on our own growth but done up to win the approval of visitors from metropolitan areas.

The above quotation addresses the issue that the absence of certain elements of a Guyanese culture has left Guyana exposed to the infiltration of metropolitan cultural pattern and trends. The Amerindian, East Indian, and African elements of culture have been allowed to grow cold. As a result, the Guyanese adopt metropolitan dress, types of entertainment, standards of beauty, and religion. All cultural standards in Guyana are measured according to the situation in the metropolitan countries. The image of cold, impotent ash is used to provide a vivid picture of the significance of the proverb. Hot ashes commands respect, while cold ash is trampled on. This proverb, *Ashij kool daag lai dong*, summarizes the situation and in its own way passes judgment upon it and characterizes its essence.

More often than not *Faa apa mek ookroo drai a trii* (Being far apart causes the okra to dry on the tree). The Okra is a delicate vegetable which perishes easily if conditions are inopportune to harvest the crop. This proverb could be applicable to a situation in which a very intelligent person fails to attain a certain level of educational development because of lack of opportunity. In this instance lack of opportunity prohibits development. This proverb can be applied to the Africans who came to Guyana during slavery, many of whom were princes and princesses in their own land. These figures would have developed their talents to govern their people, but their potential was unexplored in the West Indies slave society. This is further attested by the fact that after the Act of Emancipation the ex-slaves were able to create a new civilization, the village system, showing a genius for cooperative enterprise. If they had been in Africa or if they had had the old plantations to manage, their natural abilities would have had expression. This proverb shows that lack of opportunity can be a hindrance to growth.

The disparity of economic circumstances between the developed and the underdeveloped world portrays that *Wa dok a beed wid foul waant fo drink* (What the duck is bathing with, the fowl wants it to drink). This proverb is applicable in a situation in which the poor need money for basic necessities like food, while the rich can afford to spend theirs on luxury items. It can also apply on the international level to countries in the developed world which spend billions on space explorations while poor, underdeveloped nations are in dire need of money for basic things like food, portable water and housing.

In the Guyana context the expression *Mongkii mek ii piknii til ii spail am* (The monkey made his children till he spoiled them) mainly refers to parents who indulge their children's every whim and desire. The message is that indulgent parents prove to be their children's downfall. This proverb seems to suggest that the indulgent parent is also the senseless one, especially in matters relating to his children. Many parents do not rebuke their children because they fear annoying them and, as a result, allow them to be spoiled.

Proverbs categorized as criticism are given in this section.

1. a) *If yu fain a gool brooch a daans haal, a daans haal yu gu laas am.*
   b) If you find a gold broach in the dance hall, you will lose it there.
   c) What you obtain easily you will lose easily.

2. a) *Ashij kool daag lai dong.*
   b) If the ash is cold, the dog will lie down.
   c) Absence of a positive movement leaves a situation open to abuse.

3. a) *Faa apaa mek okroo drai a trii.*
   b) Being far apart causes the okra to dry on the tree.
   c) Lack of opportunity interferes with people's development.

4. a) *Wa dok a beed wid foul waant fo drink.*
   b) What the duck bathes with the fowl wants to drink.
   c) What some people are abusing is that of which others are in dire need.

5. a) *Stoon de batam riba ii na noo ou son at.*
   b) The stone at the bottom of the river does not know how hot the sun is.
   c) Those who are rich do not know the sufferings of the poor.

6. a) *Bok a pleza ii benab a bon.*
   b) While the buck is enjoying himself his *benab* is burning.
   c) While you are enjoying yourself your home or business is being destroyed.

7. a) *Yu doo gud yu hool wud.*
    b) If you do good, you will hold wood.
    c) The good you do is repaid by ingratitude.

8. a) *Na sii ting a dee an tek faia tik fo luk fo am a nait.*
    b) Do not see something in the day and take a fire-stick to look for it in the night.
    c) It is unwise to be in a position to achieve something good, spurn that opportunity, and then strive after the same good when circumstances are very disadvantageous.

9. a) *Yu kyaan ge spuun an bon yu haan.*
    b) You cannot have a spoon and burn your hand.
    c) If you have somebody to do something for you, you need not do it yourself.

10. a) *Yu kyaan gi wee yu batii and shit truu yu ribz'*
    b) You cannot give away your behind and defecate through your ribs.
    c) Do not give away what you need.

11. a) *Ekspiiriins gu tiich yu sens.*
    b) Experience will teach you sense.
    c) You will learn by your mistakes.

12. a) *Griidii maan doz beks tuu taim fo ii oon an fo ii matii oon.*
    b) A greedy man is annoyed twice—for his own and for his friend's own.
    c) Greedy people like to covet what belongs to others.

13. a) *Gudnis mek krapoo in ga teel tudee.*
    b) Goodness caused the *crapaud* not to have a tail today.
    c) The good you do is often repaid by ingratitude.

14. a) *Mongkii mek ii piknii til ii spail am.*
    b) The monkey made his child till he spoiled it.
    c) Indulgent parents are their children's downfall.

15. a) *Wen figz in siizn bluusakii gye fiis.*
    b) When figs are in season the blue-sackie gets a feast.
    c) People love to abuse their privileges.

16. a) *Beta belii bus dan gud bittl waas.*
    b) It is better for one's belly to burst than to allow good food (*brittle*) to be wasted.
    c) Overindulgence is sometimes permissible.

17. a) *Yu kyan tek maan outa di guta but yu kyaan tek di guta outa maan.*
    b) You can take a man/woman out of the gutter, but you can not take the gutter out of the man/woman.
    c) One cannot be expected to act out of character.

18. a) *Mi nevu tel ii se ii yai red.*
    b) I never told him that his eyes were red.
    c) I did nothing to incur his/her wrath.

19. a) *Maan ded gras groo a ii doo.*
    b) If a man is dead the grass will grow at his door.
    c) Once authority is absent, subordinates do what they please.

20. a) *Kou noo wich fence fo jump oova.*
    b) A cow knows where the fence is weak to jump over.
    c) Many take advantage of the vulnerability of others.

21. a) *Monkii noo wich lim fu klaim on.*
    b) A monkey knows on which limb to climb.
    c) Persons will take advantage of the weakest part of a system

22. a) *Pat tel pat ii batam blak.*
    b) One pot tells another pot that its bottom is black.
    c) Don't criticize others when you are guilty of the same short comings.

23. a) *Dresa faal dong maaga daag laaf*
    b) When the dresser falls down the skinny dog laughs.
    c) A poor person will rejoice at another's misfortune if he/she stands to gain.

24. a) *Dressa faal dong magga daag dkaim.*
    b) When the dresser falls down, the lean and hungry dog will climb up.
    c) A poor person will rejoice and take advantage of a rich person's misfortune.

25. a) *If yu kil piknii gi muma, muma won iit, bot if yu kil muma gi piknii, piknii wil iit.*
    b) If you kill the child and give to the mother, the mother won't eat, but if you kill the mother and give to the child, the child would eat.
    c) Children often show ingratitude.

26. a) *Ram goot se, beta ii muuma ded befoo aftnuum reen wet ii.*
    b) Billy goat says he would rather have his mother die than be caught out in the rain in the evening.
    c) Self-centered persons focus on their petty concerns and are indifferent to the problems of even their closest relatives.

27. a) *Waan from waan lef nat a faart.*
    b) One from one leaves not a fart.
    c) You are equated with nothing.

28. a) *Kyat draiv rat, bot ii a tiif ii masa fish.*
    b) Although the cat drives the rat yet he steals his master's fish.
    c) From the same source comes good and evil.

29. a) *Yu kyaan fatn kao fa anada bucha.*
     b) You cannot fatten a cow for another butcher.
     c) Guard your possessions carefully lest another steals them.

30. a) *Fish a plee a sii ii na noo wata a bail fa am.*
     b) While the fish is playing in the sea, he does not know that the water is boiling for him.
     c) Danger may be brewing while you are socializing.

31. a) *Wen galin sii fish ii fogyet se gun de.*
     b) When the galling sees fish, he forgets that the gun is there.
     c) Sometimes when one is enjoying one's self one forgets to be cautious.

32. a) *Boot gaan a faal ii kyaan kom bak.*
     b) The boat which has gone to the waterfall cannot return.
     c) Some things, once set in motion, may be difficult to change.

33. a) *Weesful maan monii gu laik buta in di son.*
     b) A wasteful man's money goes like butter in the sun.
     c) Exercise caution in financial matters.

34. a) *A mout a maan tek an koort uman, a seem mout ii a tek an put um a doo.*
     b) That same mouth which the man took to court the woman, it is that same mouth which he will take and put her out of the door.
     c) The love shown during courtship may eventually give way to bitterness and lead to divorce.

GLOSSARY OF CREOLE WORDS IN THE PROVERBS

A

accourie: a small, rodent-like animal which runs very quickly.

B

backside:	buttocks.
bake:	pancake.
battie:	buttocks
behind:	buttocks.
benab:	Amerindian home.
bittle:	food.
blue-sackie:	a bird
buck:	Amerindian (native Indian to Guyana).

C

cab horse:	horse which draws a cart.
calabash:	gourd, gourd-bearing tree.
cane knot:	joint of cane.
caterpillar:	a type of spinach.
company:	friends
crapaud:	frog.
Creole:	speakers of creole language.
curry:	a stew made with chicken and curry powder.
cutlass:	large knife, machete.

D

dam:	mud road.
dresser:	kitchen table on which meals are kept.
dutty:	mud, a wheelbarrow of loose earth.

E

estate: a type of plantation.

F

fasten:	to become stuck.
fetch:	carry.
fig:	small banana.
fire-stick:	lighted firewood.
fowl-cock:	rooster.
fufu:	pounded plantains.

G

gutter:	slum.
galling:	a sea bird.

H

hog:	female pig, sow.
hori:	freshwater fish.

51

J

jackass: donkey.

jail: prison.

K

knot: joint of (cane).

kongatee: plantain flour, plantain meal, or cassava meal. It is usually made from dried and pounded plantain or cassava. This is also called *kongwintee*. This meal can be used to make an African dish called *coo-coo*.

L

laba: small, rodent-like animal.

lick: strike, hit, beat.

leakyship: not seaworthy or trustworthy.

M

magga: lean, skinny, meager.

massa: used to refer to white plantation owners. This contraction was used up to the early twentieth century but has practically disappeared now.

matty: close friend.

O

obeah: working evil against someone.

P

patwa: freshwater fish.

pickney: used to refer to children. This is a variant of the African pickaninny.

posie: potty.

poulder: irrigation dam.

S

skin-teeth: act of grinning.

stop-off: a wooden or mud wall used to prevent erosion by river or canal.

sunfish: freshwater fish.

V

vex: to be angry.

W

water-muma: water-mother, mermaid.

Notes

Introduction

1. Martha Warren Beckwith. *Jamaica proverbs* New York: (Negro University Press, 1968) 100.
Guyanese proverbs were observed to have the same pattern, although not on all occasions.

2. By creole is meant a language which has evolved from a pidgin. A pidgin is a contact vernacular, normally not the native language of any of its speakers. It usually arises and is used in trading or in a situation which requires communication between people who speak mutually unintelligible languages. Pidgin languages have a limited vocabulary, grammatical features, and few redundant features. When the syntax and vocabulary of a pidgin are extended and it becomes the native language of a community, it has evolved into a creole.
    The term *creole* was applied to certain languages spoken by "creoles" in and around the Caribbean and in West Africa and was later extended to other languages synonymous to these types. Creole languages differ in relation to the territory and even the geographic area in which they are spoken. These differences depend to a great extent on the various European cultures that dominated the territories. However, all creole languages have the unique characteristic of combining vocabularies of European origins with grammatical structures that are of a non-European and seemingly West African nature. See Dell Hymes, *Pidginization and Creolization of Languages*.

Chapter three

[1] Beckwith (1968)

Chapter four

1. S.W. Anand Prahlad (Dennis Folly), "'No Guts, No Glory'" Proverbs, Vales and Image among Anglo-American University students.'" Southern Folklore, 51 No. 3 (1994) 285-298.
2. Marjorie Bard (1992) has called the phenomenon of using proverbs as internal dialogues "idionarration." She sees this usage of proverbs as receiving little attention.

Chapter six

1. Donald Light, Jr., and Suzanne Keller, *Sociology*. 4th ed. Knopff, 1985, 18.
2. ASCRIA, *Teachings of the Cultural Revolution* Georgetown, Guyana: (September 29, 1968), 1.

Bibliography

Abrams, Ovid S. *Guyana, Mete Gee.* Republic Issue, Labor Advocate Job Printing Department, 1970.

Allsopp, Richard A. "Folklore in Guyana Building a Guyanese Tradition." In Kyk-Over-Al edited by A.J. Seymour, 37-44. (1967).

ASCRIA. *Teachings of the Cultural Revolution.* Georgetown, Guyana: (September 29, 1968).

Bard, Marjorie. "Relating Intrapersonal Storying (Idionarrating) and Interpersonal Communicating." *Southern Folklore* 49: (1992) 61-72.

Cassidy, Frederick. *Jamaica Talk: Three Hundred Years of the English Language in Jamaica.* London: Macmillian & Co., 1961.

Hymes, D., ed. *Pidginization and Creolization of Languages.* Cambridge: Cambridge University Press, 1971.

Lawrence, Steve. *Interpretations of Commonly Used Guyanese Creole Proverbs.* Unpublished Bachelor of Arts Thesis, University of Guyana, 1972.

Light, Donald, Jr., and Suzanne Keller, *Sociology,* 4th ed. New York: Knopff, 1985.

Solomon, Victorine R. *A Study of Some Guyanese Creole Proverbs.* Unpublished Bachelor of Arts Thesis, University of Guyana, (1974).

Speirs, James. *The Proverbs of British Guiana.* Georgetown, Guyana: Demerara, 1902.

Watson, Lewellyn. *Jamaica Sayings.* Florida University Press, 1991.

Index

2772642

Made in the USA